C000186229

IT'S Cocktail TIME!

summersdale

IT'S COCKTAIL TIME!

An Hachette UK Company
www.hachette.co.uk

Summersdale Publishers Ltd
Part of Octopus Publishing Group Limited
Carmelite House
50 Victoria Embankment
LONDON
EC4Y 0DZ
UK

www.summersdale.com

Printed and bound in the Czech Republic

ISBN: 978-1-78685-519-0

Substantial discounts on bulk quantities of Summersdale books are available to corporations, professional associations and other organisations. For details contact general enquiries: telephone: +44 (0) 1243 771107 or email: enquiries@summersdale.com.

To...

From...................................

WHAT IS A *cocktail?*

The official definition of a cocktail, according to the modern Merriam-Webster dictionary, is 'a usually iced drink of wine or distilled liquor [spirit] mixed with flavouring ingredients'. Strictly speaking, a cocktail should be any drink that contains two or more ingredients, with at least one of those ingredients being alcohol.

When a cocktail contains only a distilled spirit and a liqueur it is a duo; when you add a mixer it's a trio. Additional ingredients in cocktails could be any type of fruit, sugar, syrup, honey, milk or cream, or various herbs and spices. The finishing touches, garnishes and decorations can be anything from the ubiquitous paper umbrellas, to fruit slices, spirals and twists, to herb sprigs and salt or sugar on the rim.

HISTORY OF
cocktails

There's a debate about where the word 'cocktail' comes from. The first written references date back to the late eighteenth and early nineteenth centuries, including an 1803 article in a New England publication, *The Farmer's Cabinet*, where a man says he 'drank a glass of cocktail – excellent for the head'.

Some claim that a female innkeeper in America during the revolutionary war decorated some drinks with the tail feathers of her English neighbour's chicken, which she had just cooked and served to American and French soldiers. This bold move was cheered on by her patrons, who raised their glasses to the words of '*Vive le cocktail!*'

Another story claims that the name derives from the French word *coquetier*, meaning egg cup, as a Frenchman in New Orleans was said to have served a medicinal mixed drink in egg cups in the early 1800s.

The cocktails we know and love today really all started when Prohibition was introduced in the USA in 1920. The banning of alcohol led to illegal alcohol factories springing up everywhere. Most of the spirits produced in these factories tasted awful and were sometimes even poisonous!

During this time, speakeasies – illicit bars – became very popular, as the bartenders would often mix alcohol with a number of other ingredients like cream or juice both to hide it from the police and to disguise the unpleasant taste of the poor-quality alcohol. Inevitably, mixed drinks and cocktails soared in popularity.

Whatever the word's origins really are, there's no doubt that the cocktail has played a big role in American social history. After Prohibition ended in 1933, bartenders and mixologists were free to really experiment with spirits and liqueurs, and the popularity of cocktails continues to this day. From sweet, tropical blends to modern-day craft cocktails containing novel ingredients and complex flavours, it seems we can't get enough of them.

With a trend towards greater refinement in drinking culture, cocktails have now become a central theme for a night out rather than just part of one. They're also great for a night in with friends or even an accompaniment with dinner.

THE EQUIPMENT
you'll need

If you feel overwhelmed at the thought of trying to recreate cocktails at home that you may have enjoyed in a bar, don't be. Mixing up some great cocktails is not actually as hard as it looks if you invest in the right tools – and it can be a lot of fun!

COCKTAIL SHAKER
There are a number of different shakers to choose from, including the French style, Boston shaker and Cobbler. The bartenders' favourite tends to be the Boston shaker.

FOOD PROCESSOR OR BLENDER
Useful if you want to make frozen cocktails or smoothies.

BAR SPOON
A metal spoon with a long, often twisted, shaft.

JIGGER

A two-sided shot measurer; one end holds up to 25 ml and the other 50 ml. The best jiggers on the market are those with measurement markers lower than 25 and 50 ml displayed on the inside.

MUDDLER

A stirring rod, usually metal, with a ridged circular end that is used for crushing solid ingredients.

FINE STRAINER

An item similar to an everyday kitchen sieve, only smaller and with finer holes.

ICE BUCKET
(IF YOU'RE HOSTING A BIG PARTY)

Whenever it's cocktail time, ensure you have plenty of ice. No one wants tepid drinks! Using ice is required for all the recipes in the book, so make sure you stock up.

LEMON AND LIME SQUEEZER

Varieties OF COCKTAIL GLASSES

Avoid a cocktail party faux pas by ensuring you have the appropriate glass for the drinks you serve. Here's a brief guide...

THE COCKTAIL (OR MARTINI) GLASS
Ideal for: varieties of Martinis such as Vodka Martinis and many classic cocktails such as Manhattans.

THE HIGHBALL AND COLLINS GLASSES
Ideal for: tall mixed drinks or 'Highballs', such as gin and tonic. These drinks are generally built in the glass and poured over ice. The Collins glass tends to be taller and narrower, and was traditionally used for Tom Collins cocktails.

THE OLD-FASHIONED (OR ROCKS OR 'LOWBALL') GLASS
Ideal for: short drinks served over ice, such as a White Russian (p.14).

THE SHOT GLASS

Ideal for: shots of pretty much any spirit or liqueur. However, they can also be used for mixed shooters such as the B-52 (p.41). These glasses come in a number of different shapes and sizes but all have a thick, heavy base that can withstand being slammed down on a table or bar!

THE MARGARITA GLASS

Ideal for: Margaritas (p.64), although you can easily serve them in traditional cocktail glasses too. The Margarita glass has a double bowl shape and the wide rim makes it especially easy to add salt or sugar to. These glasses also work particularly well if you're making frozen Margaritas.

THE CHAMPAGNE FLUTE

Ideal for: champagne or Prosecco cocktails such as Buck's Fizz (p.91) and Bellinis (p.22).

THE WINE GLASS

Ideal for: Sangria (p.81) and Aperol Spritz (p.47).

HOW TO MAKE COCKTAILS LIKE
a mixologist

You don't have to impersonate Tom Cruise in *Cocktail* to look like a pro, but here are some top techniques to impress your friends with...

MUDDLE
This is a way of crushing various ingredients to allow flavours, such as sugar, soft fruits, citrus fruits or mint, to infuse. Press the muddler down in a grinding motion to break down the ingredients.

STRAIN
This technique helps to sieve out any excess solids from cocktails, such as sugar, to produce a smoother texture. For best results use a fine strainer.

SHAKE
This is a popular technique to mix ingredients. Place ice into your shaker with the ingredients, tighten

the lid and apply all your effort into the shaking motion. When the shaker has formed condensation and become ice cold you know that the cocktail is ready to be decanted into a glass for serving.

STIR
Some cocktails should never be shaken because the process forms bubbles that can detract from the appearance and texture of the cocktail. Use a bar spoon to stir ingredients in steady circular motions. For all the ingredients to mix properly this technique usually takes longer than shaking (approx. 60 seconds).

LAYER
Use this technique when the recipe requires ingredients to be added in a certain order. For perfect results, ensure that the glass and ingredients are chilled, and the shots are always poured over the back of a spoon to help keep the layers separate.

Cocktail party
THEMES AND DECORATIONS

If you're having a party, a special theme is a great way to get your guests in the mood. You might also want to think about a memento for party-goers to take home at the end of the night. To get you started, there are craft ideas as well as some great theme and cocktail suggestions scattered throughout the book.

White Russian

The Black Russian cocktail, which first appeared in 1949, becomes a White Russian with the addition of cream. Neither drink is Russian in origin, but both are named due to vodka being the main ingredient.

INGREDIENTS

50 ml vodka
50 ml coffee liqueur
50 ml full fat milk
   or double cream

METHOD

Divide eight ice cubes between the two old-fashioned glasses.

Add the vodka, coffee liqueur and the milk or cream to a shaker filled with ice, put the lid on and shake until condensation forms on the outside.

Strain the mixture over the ice in the glasses and serve.

I'VE RARELY MET

A COCKTAIL

I DIDN'T LIKE.

TIM BARRETT

NOW IS THE TIME FOR DRINKING, NOW THE TIME TO DANCE FOOTLOOSE UPON THE EARTH.

HORACE

BUT FIRST,

Cocktails

Cosmopolitan

(Serves 1) Glass: Martini

First created in 1970s America, the Cosmopolitan is now regarded as the epitome of style and sass.

INGREDIENTS

40 ml vodka citron
20 ml orange liqueur
20 ml cranberry juice
1 lime
Small slice of orange peel
  to garnish

METHOD

Combine the vodka citron, orange liqueur and cranberry juice in the ice-filled shaker.

Cut the lime in half and squeeze the juice into the mix.

Shake vigorously until blended.

Strain into a glass and garnish with the orange peel.

ONE TEQUILA, TWO TEQUILA, THREE TEQUILA, FLOOR.

GEORGE CARLIN

CANDY

is

DANDY

BUT

LIQUOR

is

QUICKER.

OGDEN NASH

TEA IS SO

T A M E.

A COCKTAIL
IS LOTS MORE
NAUGHTY.

RICHARD FLORANCE

Classic Bellini

(Serves 4) Glass: Champagne flute

The famous Bellini was invented in 1934 by Giuseppe Cipriani, founder of Harry's Bar in Venice.

INGREDIENTS

2 ripe peaches (peeled, halved
   and stones removed) or
   the equivalent using tinned
   peaches in their natural juice
1 bottle Prosecco, chilled

METHOD

Place the peaches in a blender and puree until totally smooth. Divide half the peach puree between four chilled champagne flutes and slowly top up with Prosecco, stirring as you pour. Leave the other half of the puree and the extra bubbly for that second glass!

1920s SPEAKEASY-STYLE
Cocktail Party

Invite your guests to come as gangsters, molls and flappers, and whether you choose to hire a venue with a bar already set up or use your own joint, get ready for a wild evening of jazz, canapés and cocktails.

Cocktail suggestions:

- **Manhattan (p.94)**
- **Classic Champagne Cocktail (p.61)**
- **French 75 (p.117)**
- **Bee's Knees (p.158)**

I DRINK TOO MUCH.
THE LAST TIME
I GAVE A URINE
SAMPLE IT HAD
AN OLIVE IN IT.

RODNEY DANGERFIELD

You are the

mint

to my

mojito

I ONLY TAKE A DRINK

ON TWO OCCASIONS –

WHEN I'M THIRSTY *and* WHEN I'M NOT.

BRENDAN BEHAN

Mojito

(Serves 1) Glass: Collins or Highball

Havana, Cuba, is the birthplace of the Mojito, one of the nation's oldest cocktails. One story traces the popular cocktail to a similar sixteenth-century drink known as 'El Draque', after Sir Francis Drake. Drake and his men were thought to have concocted the drink to cure them of sickness so they could continue to plunder Spanish ports and ships.

INGREDIENTS

8 mint leaves plus
   extra to decorate
½ lime
2 tsp cane sugar
60 ml white rum
Soda water

METHOD

Muddle the mint leaves, lime and sugar in the bottom of your glass and fill almost to the top with crushed ice.

Add the rum, stir and top up with soda water.

Decorate with sprigs of mint and serve.

NOT EVERYONE WHO DRINKS IS A POET. SOME OF US DRINK BECAUSE WE'RE NOT POETS.

DUDLEY MOORE

IT'S NEVER TOO A FOR A COCKTAIL.

NOËL COWARD

ALCOHOL

is not

THE ANSWER.

❧

IT JUST MAKES YOU

forget

THE QUESTION.

ANONYMOUS

English Garden

(Serves 1) Glass: Collins or Highball

This is a modern cocktail, reportedly invented in 2001 by London bartenders Daniel Warner and Tobias Blazquez-Garcia.

INGREDIENTS

25 ml gin
50 ml freshly squeezed
   apple juice
20 ml lime juice
20 ml sugar syrup
Sprig of mint
Slice of cucumber, plus
   extra to garnish

METHOD

Fill a cocktail shaker with ice and add the gin, apple juice, lime juice and syrup.

Add the mint and cucumber, shake again to release the new ingredients' flavours and strain into a Collins glass. Serve with a slice of cucumber.

Glow Stick Balloons

These will literally light up any party and get your guests in the mood for merriment.

WHAT YOU WILL NEED

Balloons
Glow sticks
String

METHOD

Just before your party, activate the glow sticks by bending them.

Blow up each balloon just over its natural inflated size.

While pinching the end of the balloon, take the glow stick and feed it into the balloon so it's fully inside.

Tie a knot in the balloon.

Arrange the balloons nicely and dim the lights when your guests arrive so that they can admire the dazzling colours.

WHEN I

 READ

ABOUT THE EVILS
OF DRINKING, I
GAVE UP READING.

HENNY YOUNGMAN

I HAVE TAKEN
MORE OUT OF
ALCOHOL THAN
ALCOHOL HAS
TAKEN OUT OF ME.

WINSTON CHURCHILL

KEEP

CALM

AND

DRINK

cocktails

Lemon Drop

(Serves 2) Glass: Shot glass

This popular cocktail has a number of variations, but this one is fresh and zingy and not over-sweet.

INGREDIENTS

35 ml lemon vodka
35 ml limoncello
1 dash lemon juice
1 dash lime cordial

METHOD

Put some ice cubes into a cocktail shaker, add the lemon vodka, limoncello, lemon juice and lime cordial and give it a quick shake.

Strain into glasses and serve.

IF YOU DON'T
DRINK, HOW WILL
YOUR FRIENDS
KNOW YOU
love them
AT 2 A.M.?!

ONE MORE DRINK AND I'LL BE UNDER THE .

DOROTHY PARKER

THE REALLY
IMPORTANT THINGS

ARE SAID OVER
COCKTAILS
and
ARE NEVER DONE.

PETER DRUCKER

B-52

(Serves 1) Glass: Shot glass

The name refers to the US B-52 Stratofortress – a long-range bomber. It was used in the Vietnam War for the release of incendiary bombs, and this may have inspired today's flaming variant of the cocktail.

INGREDIENTS

1 part coffee liqueur
1 part Irish cream
1 part orange liqueur

METHOD

Pour the coffee liqueur into a shot glass.

Slowly pour the Irish cream over the back of a spoon onto the coffee liqueur. Then do the same with the orange liqueur.

You should be left with three separate liqueur layers.

POUR YOURSELF
A DRINK... AND
PULL YOURSELF
TOGETHER.

ELIZABETH TAYLOR

SOMETIMES TOO MUCH TO DRINK IS BARELY .

MARK TWAIN

1980s COCKTAIL
NIGHT

Channel your inner Tom Cruise with a 1980s-inspired cocktail party. Some suggestions:

- Legwarmers (compulsory)
- Play popular 1980s tunes: think Wham!
- Provide a 'Big Hair Blowout Bar' with hairdryers, brushes and plenty of hairspray
- Decorate with glow stick balloons (see p.33) and neon lighting if the budget will stretch
- Provide glow stick bracelets for your guests

Classic 1980s cocktails include:

- Long Island Iced Tea (p.113)
- Piña Colada (p.84)
- Buck's Fizz (p.91)
- Singapore Sling (p.122)

Why limit
happy
to an
hour?

ALCOHOL

is a

MISUNDERSTOOD

VITAMIN.

P. G. WODEHOUSE

Aperol Spritz

(Serves 1) Glass: Large wine glass or Highball

Aperol Spritz became popular in the 1950s and is now considered to be Italy's drink. The low-alcohol cocktail is built around Aperol, a semi-sweet, slightly bitter aperitif from northern Italy.

INGREDIENTS

3 parts Prosecco
2 parts Aperol
1 splash soda water
Orange slice to garnish

METHOD

Add the Prosecco to your glass with plenty of ice.

Top up with the Aperol and add the splash of soda water.

Garnish with a slice of orange and serve.

SOMEONE SLIPPED A HANGOVER IN MY DRINK LAST NIGHT.

ANONYMOUS

THE FEAST OF REASON AND THE FLOW OF SOUL.

ALEXANDER POPE ON ALCOHOL

Daiquiri

(Serves 1) Glass: Martini

The Daiquiri was invented in Cuba, the home of rum. Its pure flavours have struck a chord with many, and it even got a mention in F. Scott Fitzgerald's book *This Side of Paradise*.

INGREDIENTS

1 lime
½ tsp caster sugar
70 ml white rum

METHOD

Cut the lime in half and squeeze the juice into the ice-filled shaker.

Stir in the sugar and then add the rum. If you prefer to use dark rum, make sure that you don't use as much sugar.

Give the concoction a vigorous shake and strain into the glass.

SIMPLY

ENJOY LIFE

and the

GREAT PLEASURES

THAT COME WITH IT.

KAROLÍNA KURKOVÁ

I NEVER DRINK ANYTHING STRONGER THAN GIN BEFORE BREAKFAST.

W. C. FIELDS

PIMP YOUR
PROSECCO PARTY

Make your Prosecco party even more fun by asking guests to pimp their own fizz. Ensure you provide a good selection of spirits, liqueurs, mixers and fruit for them to create their own blends.

Here are some cocktail suggestions as a guide for your guests, so you may want to make blackboard menus for:

- **Classic Bellini (p.22)**
- **French 75 (p.117)**
- **Aperol Spritz (p.47)**
- **D'Artagnan (p.75)**
- **Classic Champagne Cocktail (p.61)**

WHAT'S *drinking?*

A MERE PAUSE FROM

THINKING.

LORD BYRON

Let's have a *drink.* It's five o'clock somewhere in the *world*

Classic Martini

(Serves 1) Glass: Martini

A descendant of the sweeter Martinez cocktail, the Martini has been adapted over time more than most classic cocktails, even where the embellishments are concerned. But one question is still up for debate: is it best shaken or stirred?

INGREDIENTS

35 ml dry vermouth
120 ml gin
1 olive or cherry to garnish

METHOD

Add ice to the shaker.

Pour in the dry vermouth, stir briefly and strain.

Add the gin of your choice; a good-quality brand and strength will affect the overall quality of the drink.

Connoisseurs recommend it should be around 84-proof (47 per cent).

Then stir (or shake à la James Bond) until the shaker is cold, and strain into the glass.

Garnish with an olive, or a cherry if you're keeping things traditional.

I'M GETTING

cultured –

ONE COCKTAIL

AT A TIME

THERE ARE TWO

OF PEOPLE I DON'T
TRUST: PEOPLE
WHO DON'T DRINK
AND PEOPLE WHO
COLLECT STICKERS.

CHELSEA HANDLER

ON FRIDAYS
I PREFER MY
ESPRESSO IN A
Martini

Classic Champagne Cocktail

(Serves 1) Glass: Champagne flute

There are many variations of this famous cocktail, but this is the classic way to add a little more sparkle to your French fizz.

INGREDIENTS

1 white sugar cube
2 dashes Angostura bitters
20 ml cognac
Champagne, chilled

METHOD

Place the sugar cube onto a dessert spoon and pour the bitters directly over it.

Drop the soaked sugar cube into a chilled champagne flute and add the cognac.

Top up the glass with champagne and serve.

TO ME, 'DRINK RESPONSIBLY' MEANS DON'T SPILL IT.

ANONYMOUS

ABSTAINER:
A WEAK PERSON *who yields* TO THE *temptation* OF DENYING HIMSELF A
PLEASURE.

AMBROSE BIERCE

Margarita

(Serves 1) Glass: Margarita or Martini

The Margarita was the first cocktail made with tequila as its main alcohol-based component – a daring tipple that hailed from Mexico.

INGREDIENTS

Lime wedge, plus one to garnish
Salt
35 ml tequila
20 ml triple sec
20 ml fresh lime juice

METHOD

Circle the rim of the glass with the lime wedge and put the glass face down onto a layer of salt, leaving it long enough so the salt sticks.

Pour the tequila, triple sec and lime juice into a shaker filled with ice.

Shake well and strain into a glass.

Place a lime wedge on the rim of the glass. Salud!

To make a frozen Margarita, blend the tequila, triple sec and lime juice together with a handful of ice on high speed until it turns into slush.

'TRUST ME,
YOU CAN
DANCE.'
Margarita

Flute Tags

This is a great way of labelling drinks decoratively.

WHAT YOU WILL NEED

Coloured paper
Scissors
Hole-punch
Different coloured pens

METHOD

Cut shapes out of your
coloured paper depending
on your chosen cocktail party
theme (hearts always work well).

Punch a circle close to one of the tag's
edges. Then cut a slit from the closest
edge to the hole so the tags can be easily
attached to the glass stem when needed.

Place your tags near the flutes along with
an assortment of pens. Let your guests
personalise their tags so they can easily
identify their glass throughout the night.

I DON'T HAVE A DRINKING PROBLEM 'CEPT WHEN I CAN'T GET ANOTHER .

TOM WAITS

DRINK BECAUSE YOU ARE HAPPY, BUT NEVER BECAUSE YOU ARE MISERABLE.

G. K. CHESTERTON

HERE'S TO

ALCOHOL,

the

ROSE-COLOURED GLASSES

 ## OF LIFE.

F. SCOTT FITZGERALD

Sloe Gin Fizz

(Serves 1) Glass: Highball or Sling

Sloe gin is so popular in the UK that there are several competitions and awards dedicated to it, including the Sloe Gin World Championships in East Sussex.

INGREDIENTS

60 ml sloe gin
30 ml freshly squeezed
    lemon/lime juice
1 tsp sugar syrup
Soda water
Slice of lemon to garnish

METHOD

Shake the gin, lemon/lime juice and sugar syrup over ice in a shaker.

Strain the mix into an ice-filled glass. Top up with the soda water and stir.

Garnish with a slice of lemon.

I NEVER DRINK
WATER; THAT
IS THE STUFF
THAT RUSTS
.

W. C. FIELDS

IF YOU OBEY ALL THE RULES YOU MISS ALL THE FUN.

KATHARINE HEPBURN

COCKTAILS ARE ALWAYS THE *answer*

D'Artagnan

(Serves 1) Glass: Champagne flute

Named after d'Artagnan, the fourth musketeer, this drink is a celebration of chivalry and friendship.

INGREDIENTS

1 tsp Armagnac
1 tsp orange liqueur
3 tsp chilled orange juice
½ tsp simple sugar syrup
Champagne or Prosecco, chilled
Orange twist to garnish

METHOD

Pour all the ingredients, apart from the fizz, into a chilled champagne flute.

Stir gently, then top up with champagne or Prosecco and garnish with an orange twist.

Disco Ball Cocktail Stirrer

This is a great craft idea if you are bored on a rainy day. Once made, they can be reused again and again.

WHAT YOU WILL NEED

Ping-pong ball
Metal skewer
5mm-square mirror
  mosaic tiles
Glue
Bamboo stick, cut to the correct
  length to fit inside the glass

METHOD

Pierce the ping-pong ball (very carefully!) using the skewer to make a hole the size of the end of the bamboo stick.

If your tiles are not self-adhesive, glue
each tile onto the ball without
covering the hole and leave
to dry.

Once dry, fit the ball onto the
end of the bamboo stick and
fix with glue to secure properly.
Leave for several hours to dry.

Cocktails and dreams

TONIGHT'S FORECAST: 99 PER CENT CHANCE OF *Cocktails*

ALCOHOL IS THE
ANAESTHESIA

BY WHICH WE ENDURE

THE OPERATION
OF LIFE.

GEORGE BERNARD SHAW

Sangria

(Serves 10–12) Glass: Wine

From humble roots, this Spanish drink really packs a punch at a party.

INGREDIENTS

2 bottles light Spanish red
    wine, chilled
125 ml brandy
Orange, lemon and
    apple wedges
Cinnamon stick plus extra
    for garnish
Lemonade, chilled
Lemon slices to garnish

METHOD

Put a generous amount of ice cubes in a large jug, then add the wine, brandy, fruit wedges and one cinnamon stick and stir together.

When you're ready to serve, top up the jug with lemonade, stir and pour. Garnish each glass with a slice of lemon and a cinnamon stick.

HEALTH – WHAT MY FRIENDS ARE ALWAYS DRINKING TO BEFORE THEY FALL .

PHYLLIS DILLER

I WANT MY TOES IN THE SAND AND *a cocktail in hand*

Piña Colada

(Serves 1) Glass: Highball

The first printed reference to the Piña Colada cocktail in a 1906 issue of *The Washington Post* dubbed it *piña fria* (cold pineapple), as it didn't contain rum or coconut milk. Thankfully, it's now very much an alcoholic drink.

INGREDIENTS

50 ml pineapple juice
45 ml white rum
50 ml coconut cream
Two triangles of pineapple
   to garnish

METHOD

Mix all the liquid ingredients in a shaker and add ice.

Shake vigorously until the mix is a consistent texture and strain the concoction into the glass.

Make a slit down the middle of both pineapple chunks and wedge onto the rim of the glass.

For the full beach holiday experience, why not serve this in half a hollowed-out pineapple?

THERE'S NOTHING WRONG WITH SOBRIETY IN MODERATION.

JOHN CIARDI

When
all
else fails...
Cocktails

LET THE FUN
BE-GIN!

If you haven't noticed already, the popularity of gin has soared over the past few years and it shows no signs of stopping – and for good reason. So invite your guests to a fun night of mixing cocktails with this beautiful, botanical-infused spirit. You may want to source one of the many varieties of flavoured gins to add even more interest to your gin-based cocktails.

Here are some you'll find in this book:

- Bramble (p.109)
- English Garden (p.32)
- Bee's Knees (p.158)
- Sloe Gin Fizz (p.71)
- Camomile and Gin (p.136)

I DRINK WHEN

I have

OCCASION

~·~°~·~

AND SOMETIMES WHEN I HAVE

Nᵒ OCCASION.

MIGUEL DE CERVANTES

SIP, SIP,
hooray!

Buck's Fizz

(Serves 4) Glass: Champagne flute

This cocktail is traditionally served on Christmas morning or at a pre-wedding breakfast, but who needs a celebration to enjoy this simple yet delicious drink?

INGREDIENTS

1 bottle champagne or
   Prosecco, chilled
Large carton orange juice

METHOD

In four chilled champagne flutes, mix two parts fizz with one part orange juice.

ALCOHOL, TAKEN
IN SUFFICIENT
QUANTITIES, MAY

ALL THE EFFECTS
OF DRUNKENNESS.

OSCAR WILDE

IT'S BEGINNING

TO LOOK A

LOT LIKE

Cocktails

Manhattan

(Serves 1) Glass: Martini

The Manhattan is said to be one of the most harmonious cocktails for flavours, alongside the Martini.

INGREDIENTS

70 ml whisky (rye or bourbon)
35 ml sweet vermouth
2–3 dashes aromatic bitters
1 cherry or small slice of lemon
    peel to garnish

METHOD

Pour the whisky (rye is recommended but bourbon is fine if preferred), vermouth and bitters into the ice-filled shaker.

Stir lightly and carefully, but well. Shaking will make the cocktail cloudy to the eye and oily to the taste.

Strain the drink into the glass and garnish with the lemon peel or cherry.

THE MANHATTAN,
THE DRY GIN MARTINI
AND THE NEGRONI COULD
BE CONSIDERED THE
TRIPLE CROWN OF THE
COCKTAIL KINGDOM.

GARY REGAN

There's always

time

for a

cocktail

Jewelled Canvas Bag

These take a little while to make so only give them as a takeaway if you're hosting a small get-together. You could even surprise your guests with a gift inside the bags.

WHAT YOU NEED

Plain canvas bags
Pencil
Template of a cocktail glass
Sequins and gems
Jewel glue

METHOD

On the canvas bag, stencil around the cocktail glass template; there is a whole range of templates that you can print out on the internet.

Then apply the sequins and gems to the bag using jewel glue, filling in the outline of the glass. One effective colour scheme is to use only one colour, but start with a dark shade at the bottom and gradually get lighter.

TEETOTALLERS

lack the

SYMPATHY

and

GENEROSITY

of men that

 DRINK.

W. H. DAVIES

DRINK! FOR YOU KNOW NOT WHENCE YOU CAME NOR WHY: DRINK! FOR YOU KNOW NOT WHY YOU GO, NOR .

OMAR KHAYYAM

Tom Collins

(Serves 1) Glass: Collins

The Tom Collins was one of the first cocktails to come onto the party scene. It was thought to have been invented in the early 1800s by a London bartender, and was originally given his own name, John Collins.

INGREDIENTS

60 ml dry gin
30 ml fresh lemon juice
1 tsp caster sugar
Dash of soda water
Cherry to garnish
Orange slice to garnish

METHOD

Add the gin, lemon juice and sugar to a shaker filled with ice and shake well.

Strain the mixture into the glass.

Top up with soda water and stir.

Garnish with the cherry and the orange slice, squeezing the orange first to release a zesty flavour.

COCKTAILS:
THE REASON
TO GET OUT
OF BED EVERY
afternoon

I DRINK TO MAKE OTHER PEOPLE MORE INTERESTING.

ERNEST HEMINGWAY

Whisky Sour

(Serves 1) Glass: Old-Fashioned

The Whisky Sour was first officially mentioned in Jerry Thomas's *Bartender's Guide* in 1862.

INGREDIENTS

1 tsp caster sugar
60 ml whisky (rye or bourbon)
30 ml fresh lemon juice
½ egg white (optional)
Maraschino cherry to garnish
Slice of orange peel to garnish

METHOD

Dissolve the sugar in the whisky by stirring in a shaker mixed with ice.

Then add the lemon juice and egg white (optional) and shake vigorously. If adding egg white, make sure you shake the mixture at least a minute longer in order to create a thick texture.

Garnish with a cherry and an orange peel held over a flame for a couple of seconds.

KNOCK,
KNOCK,
IT'S

cocktail
o'clock

WHEN I DRINK

I THINK

and

WHEN I THINK

I DRINK.

FRANÇOIS RABELAIS

Gym?
I thought
you said
gin!

Bramble

(Serves 1) Glass: Old-Fashioned

Dick Bradsell, the legendary London bartender and inventor of the Bramble, also created other classics such as the Espresso Martini and Russian Spring Punch.

INGREDIENTS

60 ml gin
30 ml freshly squeezed
    lemon juice
15 ml sugar syrup
15 ml crème de mure
Blackberries to garnish

METHOD

Fill an old-fashioned glass with crushed ice and add the gin, lemon juice and sugar syrup.

Top with more crushed ice and pour the crème de mure over the top. Garnish with a couple of blackberries.

1970s DISCO
Fever

Dust down the glitterball, grab a copy of *Saturday Night Fever* and get your guests to don their flares! There are some great 1970s-inspired cocktails and snacks you could serve too – cheese and pineapple on sticks, cocktail sausages, olives or, if you want to push the boat out, how about a fondue? Some popular cocktail choices during this decade included:

- **Sloe Gin Fizz (p.71)**
- **Singapore Sling (p.122)**
- **Tom Collins (p.100)**
- **White Russian (p.14)**
- **Kamikaze (p.127)**

THE ONLY TIME I EVER ENJOYED IRONING WAS THE DAY I ACCIDENTALLY GOT GIN IN THE STEAM .

A PENNY
SAVED IS
A COCKTAIL
earned

Long Island Iced Tea

(Serves 2) Glass: Highball

Because of the cola this cocktail can be deceptive. It's delicious but laden with liqueurs and spirits, so best stick to one glass!

INGREDIENTS

25 ml vodka
25 ml gin
25 ml white rum
25 ml tequila
25 ml orange liqueur
25 ml fresh lemon juice
Cola to top up
Lemon slices to garnish

METHOD

Put the vodka, gin, rum, tequila, orange liqueur and lemon juice in a cocktail shaker along with some ice cubes and shake.

Strain into two glasses filled with ice cubes and top up with cola.

Decorate with a slice of lemon and serve.

ALCOHOL MAY
NOT SOLVE YOUR
PROBLEMS, BUT
NEITHER WILL
WATER OR MILK.

ANONYMOUS

THE CHURCH IS NEAR

BUT THE ROAD IS ICY.

THE BAR IS

FAR AWAY

BUT I WILL WALK

CAREFULLY.

PROVERB

French 75

(Serves 4) Glass: Champagne flute

The kick of the alcohol in this Parisian cocktail is said to feel like being shelled by the French 75-mm field gun used in World War One.

INGREDIENTS

120 ml gin
60 ml freshly squeezed
    lemon juice
Icing sugar
1 bottle champagne or
    Prosecco, chilled
Lemon twist to garnish

METHOD

Mix the gin, lemon juice and sugar together.

Spoon some crushed ice into four flutes and divide the mix between them.

Then fill to the top with fizz.

Garnish with a twist of lemon.

WHEN LIFE GIVES YOU PINEAPPLES,

just add rum

Cocktail Umbrella Wreath

A fun way to greet your guests as they arrive for cocktails is to hang a paper umbrella wreath at your door. It's so simple to make too.

WHAT YOU WILL NEED

Lots of paper umbrellas
Foam wreath (from a hobby/
   crafting store)
Coloured string or ribbon

METHOD

Open all the umbrellas and group them by colour.

Secure the umbrellas on the front of the wreath by sticking their wooden stems directly into the foam evenly, colour by colour. When you hang the wreath, the tops of the umbrellas should be facing outwards.

Loop some string or ribbon around and display on your door.

 **OR BLOTTO, THIS IS YOUR MOTTO: KEEP MUDDLING THROUGH.**

IRA GERSHWIN

BAD MEN LIVE THAT
THEY MAY EAT AND
DRINK, WHEREAS GOOD
MEN EAT AND DRINK
THAT THEY MAY LIVE.

SOCRATES

Singapore Sling

(Serves 1) Glass: Highball

Around a hundred years ago, a man named Ngiam Tong Boon was said to have invented the first Singapore Sling when he was working in the Long Bar at the Raffles Hotel.

INGREDIENTS

70 ml gin
15 ml cherry brandy
7 ml grenadine
7 ml Bénédictine
20 ml orange juice
15 ml fresh lime juice
2 dashes bitters
Orange slice to garnish
Maraschino cherry to garnish

METHOD

Combine all the ingredients except the garnishes in the shaker, add ice and shake until there is a significant head of foam on the concoction's surface.

Strain the mix into an ice-filled glass.

Top with a slice of orange – cut down the middle and wedged on the rim of the glass – and a cherry.

It's *Friday* and I'm *thirsty*

NEVER

TRUST A MAN

WHO DOESN'T

DRINK.

JAMES CRUMLEY

TIME TO DRINK
tequila
AND DANCE ON
THE TABLE

Kamikaze

(Serves 2) Glass: Shot glass

Born in the late 1970s during the days of disco, the Kamikaze is an easy-to-make shot that's perfect for getting the party started.

INGREDIENTS

50 ml vodka
50 ml orange liqueur
25 ml fresh lemon juice

METHOD

Put plenty of ice in the cocktail shaker with the ingredients, shake briefly and strain into two shot glasses.

 **ME DOWN IN THE BAR! WE'LL DRINK BREAKFAST TOGETHER.**

A DRINK A DAY KEEPS THE SHRINK AWAY.

EDWARD ABBEY

Personalised Sequinned Glasses

Wow your guests with glasses that bear their names and then offer them as a takeaway gift. All the equipment for these can be found in craft shops or online.

WHAT YOU WILL NEED

Cocktail glasses
Sequins and gems
Glass pens
Wood glue

METHOD

Before your party, stick the sequins and gems onto the glasses using the wood glue, or write on them if you prefer.

On your guests' arrival, fill their glasses with a delicious cocktail and let them admire their printed name on the glass.

Drinks are *best* mixed with *friends*

I DIDN'T

TEXT YOU.

Vodka

did

Tequila Sunrise

(Serves 1) Glass: Collins

This is based on the original recipe, which doesn't contain the large amount of orange juice that most people add nowadays.

INGREDIENTS

50 ml tequila
¼ lime juice
20 ml crème de cassis
Soda water
Orange slice to garnish
Maraschino cherry to garnish

METHOD

Pour the tequila, then the lime juice, over a spoon into a chilled glass.

Layer the crème de cassis on top of the other ingredients, again over a spoon.

Top up with soda water.

Garnish with an orange slice and a maraschino cherry.

MY NERVES

COULD

use a

DRINK.

GRACE KELLY

IF LIFE  YOU LIMES, MAKE MARGARITAS.

JIMMY BUFFETT

Camomile and Gin

(Serves 1) Glass: Margarita

Camomile is said to have many health benefits: it can be used to treat anything from hay fever to chickenpox!

INGREDIENTS

25 ml camomile tea
60 ml gin
25 ml pink grapefruit
   or lemon juice
Twist of lime to garnish

METHOD

Brew the tea then wait until it cools down completely.

Shake all the ingredients vigorously in a shaker with ice until mixed.

Strain into a glass and garnish with a twist of lime.

I DISTRUST CAMELS,
OR ANYONE ELSE
WHO CAN GO A WEEK
WITHOUT A DRINK.

JOE E. LEWIS

A COCKTAIL

DONE RIGHT

can really show

YOUR GUESTS

THAT YOU CARE.

DANNY MEYER

CRAFT
Cocktail Night

If you want something a little more sedate from your evening, then invite your more creative friends around for an evening of making, shaking and mixing.

A craft cocktail is one where every element is tailored specifically to the drink. You can serve them in custom glassware, poured over bespoke ice cubes and mixed with delicious home-made syrups.

Get yourself a whole assortment of glasses, spirits, liqueurs, syrups, fruits and herbs and have some fun mixing some unique craft cocktails and coming up with inventive names for them.

YOU CAN'T BUY
happiness,
BUT YOU CAN
MAKE A COCKTAIL
AND THAT'S
KIND OF THE
same thing

Negroni

(Serves 1) Glass: Highball

Traditionally served as an aperitif, the Negroni has made a comeback in recent years. Travel to Juniper, a bar in Vancouver, and you can even get it on tap.

INGREDIENTS

35 ml Campari
35 ml sweet vermouth
35 ml gin
Small slice orange peel to garnish

METHOD

Pour the ingredients into an ice-filled glass over a bar spoon.

Stir until thoroughly mixed.

Heat the slice of orange peel with a flame until juice appears and place it in the cocktail to give it a zesty kick.

BUT I'M NOT SO THINK AS YOU DRUNK I AM.

J. C. SQUIRE

REALITY IS AN ILLUSION CREATED BY A OF ALCOHOL.

ANONYMOUS

Bloody Mary

(Serves 1) Glass: Highball

A hangover remedy in its own right, this cocktail is loaded with tomatoes, which are a great source of vitamin C and glutathione (a substance that fights against nasty toxins).

INGREDIENTS

Coarse sea salt
Chilli powder
10 ml fresh lemon juice,
   plus a dab for the glass
60 ml vodka
100 ml tomato juice
5–6 dashes Worcestershire sauce
3–4 dashes tabasco
2–3 pinches black pepper
1 pinch celery salt

METHOD

Mix one part coarse sea salt and one part chilli powder on a flat surface.

Using your finger, circle the rim of the glass with lemon juice and put the glass face down onto the salt and chilli and leave for a few seconds until it sticks to the glass.

Add the vodka, tomato juice, lemon juice, Worcestershire sauce, tabasco, pepper and celery salt to a shaker filled with ice cubes and shake vigorously.

Top the glass up with whole ice cubes. The Bloody Mary is usually enjoyed as a daytime drink, so whole ice cubes will keep the cocktail cooler for longer and allow you to take your time drinking.

Strain the contents from the shaker into the glass.

I KNEW I WAS DRUNK.

I felt

SOPHISTICATED

and

COULDN'T PRONOUNCE IT.

ANONYMOUS

I have
mixed
drinks about
feelings

Ginger Snap

(Serves 1) Glass: Old-Fashioned

Something simple, slightly different and wonderfully warming for the winter months.

INGREDIENTS

75 ml vodka
25 ml ginger wine
Dash of Angostura bitters
Soda water

METHOD

Put 4–6 ice cubes into your glass.

Pour the vodka, ginger wine and Angostura bitters into your glass and stir.

Top up with soda water, and serve.

SOUP OF THE DAY:

tequila

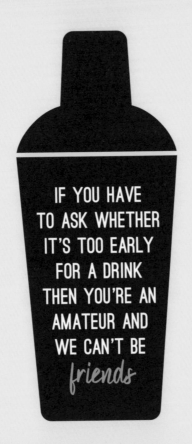

IF YOU HAVE
TO ASK WHETHER
IT'S TOO EARLY
FOR A DRINK
THEN YOU'RE AN
AMATEUR AND
WE CAN'T BE
friends

Confetti Throwers

Celebrate the success of your party by getting your guests to release the stoppers on these homemade confetti throwers, and create a room shimmering with colour.

WHAT YOU WILL NEED

Plastic tubes with stoppers
Tissue paper in various colours
Scissors or a craft hole-punch

METHOD

Using the scissors or craft hole-punch, cut or punch the tissue paper into small squares.

Fill the plastic tubes with the tissue paper, ensuring a variety of colours are used for each individual tube.

Fit the stopper in the tube, and prepare to celebrate!

Mai Tai

(Serves 1) Glass: Old-Fashioned

If you don't have an excuse to drink a Mai Tai cocktail for the other 364 days of the year, at least you do on 30 August – Hawaii's National Mai Tai Day.

INGREDIENTS

35 ml light rum
35 ml orange curaçao
17 ml orgeat syrup
Juice of a lime
35 ml dark rum
Maraschino cherry to garnish

METHOD

Pour all the ingredients except the dark rum into a shaker with ice cubes and shake well.

Strain into a glass half-full with ice.

Add the dark rum into the glass over a bar spoon to help it spread more evenly.

Garnish with the cherry.

WRITER'S BLOCK
IS A FANCY

MADE UP BY WHINERS
SO THEY CAN HAVE
AN EXCUSE TO
DRINK ALCOHOL.

STEVE MARTIN

FRIENDS ARE THERAPISTS YOU CAN *drink* *with*

Watermelon Prosecco Cocktail

(Serves 6-8) Glass: Jam Jar

The perfect summer party drink to cool down with at the end of a hot day.

INGREDIENTS

1 watermelon
200 ml vodka
1 bottle Prosecco, chilled
Fresh mint

METHOD

Peel, then chop the watermelon into chunks and pop them into the freezer, along with your bottle of vodka.

When you're ready to serve, put roughly a quarter of the watermelon chunks into a blender (you can eat the rest of the watermelon with the cocktail) along with the vodka and blitz until smooth. Top up with fizz and then blend on a low setting to combine.

Fill a large pitcher with ice, add the watermelon mixture, top up with Prosecco and garnish with plenty of fresh mint leaves.

'LET'S *FLAMINGLE*'

This tropical theme is perfect for a summer cocktail party and there are plenty of party accessories available to really make the most of the theme, such as:

- Piñatas
- Inflatables, such as palm trees, flamingos, beach balls, a mini paddling pool (perhaps filled with ice to serve as a drinks cooler)
- Buckets and spades (for snacks and nibbles)
- Beach towels draped over the chairs or deck chairs if you have them
- Paper umbrellas (for your cocktails)

Cocktail suggestions:

- Tequila Sunrise (p.133)
- Mai Tai (p.152)
- Margarita (p.64)
- A large jug of Sangria (p.81)

Bee's Knees

(Serves 1) Glass: Martini

The rumour is that this Prohibition-era cocktail was flavoured with lemon and honey to hide the taste of the bathtub gin it was made from!

INGREDIENTS

10 ml runny honey
5 ml water
50 ml gin
15 ml freshly squeezed
  lemon juice
Lemon twist to garnish

METHOD

Stir the honey into the water until blended.

Pour into a chilled cocktail glass and mix in the gin and lemon juice.

Serve with a lemon twist.

Always

LIVE LIFE WITH A COCKTAIL IN ONE HAND

If you're interested in finding out
more about our books, find us on
Facebook at **Summersdale Publishers**
and follow us on Twitter at **@Summersdale**.

www.summersdale.com

IMAGE CREDITS